AEROFILMS GUIDE

London

Iain Thomson

IAN ALLAN Publishing

London

Based on an original idea by Richard Cox
of Aerofilms

Designer Michael D. Stride
Series Editor Rebecca King

While every effort has been taken to ensure
the accuracy of the information in this
book, the publishers cannot accept
responsibility for errors or omissions, or for
changes in details given.

First published 1992

ISBN 0 7110 2040 X

Published by Ian Allan Ltd, Shepperton, Surrey;
and printed by Ian Allan Printing Ltd at their
works at Coombelands in Runnymede, England

Inset: Buckingham Palace

Looking towards Trafalgar Square

Title page:
St Paul's Cathedral
Tower Bridge

Contents

About this book

TRANSPORT

Getting round London is not as difficult as you'd think. While the transport system of train, bus and underground may be expensive and crowded to bursting during the rush hours, during the day you can take advantage of off peak fares and special daily or weekly tickets.

The photo-maps in this book identify the general locations (although not all the entrances and exits) of the underground and the railway stations. Maps of the system and details about fares can be obtained from stations, information points or:

Railways: Network SouthEast, Network House, 1 Eversholt Street, London, NW1 1DN.

Underground and Buses: London Transport, 55 Broadway, London, SW1H 0BD.

SCALE

The scale of an aerial photograph depends on the height of the area being photographed. If the land were completely flat and the scale 1:5000, then 1km would be represented by 20cm, at 1:8000 1km would be 12.5cm, and at 1:10000 it would be 10cm.

However with countryside that's hilly, the scale can vary from the top of the hill to the bottom. London is, in the main, fairly flat and the scales used therefore give an accurate indication of distance. The images portrayed give actual sizes of buildings, and widths of roads – unlike most of the city maps which have to satisfy accuracy in order to accommodate street names.

In the border, the scale of each photo-map, and a half-kilometre scale bar, are displayed.

1:10 000

1:8000

1:5000

KEY TO PHOTO-MAPS
Showing scale of each page

HAMPSTEAD
1:10 000

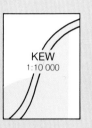

KEW
1:10 000

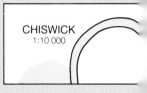

CHISWICK
1:10 000

HAMPTON
COURT
1:5000

AEROFILMS LIMITED

Aerofilms was founded in 1919 and has specialised in the acquisition of aerial photography within the United Kingdom throughout its history. The Company has a record of being innovative in the uses and applications of aerial photography.

Photographs looking at the environment in perspective are called oblique aerial photographs. These photographs are taken wit

4

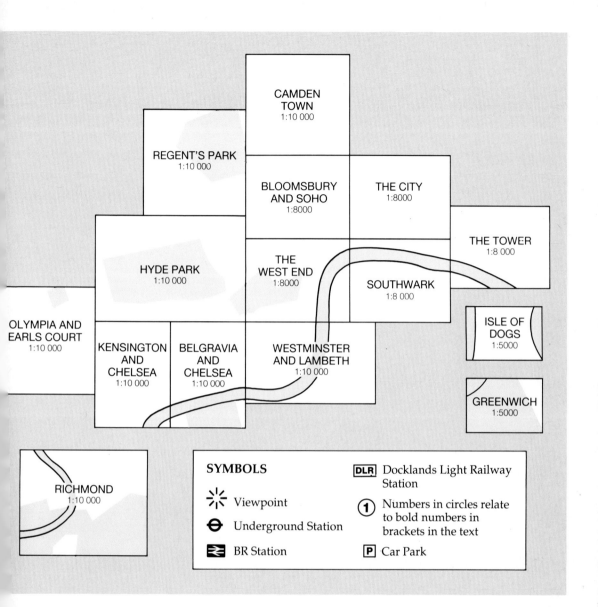

SYMBOLS

☀ Viewpoint

⊖ Underground Station

⇄ BR Station

|DLR| Docklands Light Railway Station

① Numbers in circles relate to bold numbers in brackets in the text

|P| Car Park

Hasselblad cameras by professional photographers experienced in the difficult conditions encountered in aerial work. Photographs looking straight down at the landscape are termed vertical aerial photographs. These photographs are obtained by using Leica survey cameras, the products from which are normally used in the making of maps.

Aerofilms has a unique library of oblique and vertical photographs in excess of one and one half million photographs covering the United Kingdom. This library of photographs dates from 1919 to the present and is continually being updated.

Oblique and vertical photography can be taken to customers specification by Aerofilms professional photographers. Due to the specific nature of the requirements of the Aerofilms guides, new photography has been taken for these books.

To discover more of the wealth of past or present photographs held in the library at Aerofilms, including photographs in this guide, or to commission new aerial photography to your requirements, please contact:

Aerofilms Limited
Gate Studios
Station Road
Borehamwood
Herts
WD6 1EJ

Telephone: 081-207 0666
Fax: 081-207 5433

HAMPTON COURT

HAMPTON COURT

Hampton Court lies on the banks of the Thames some 15 miles (24km) south-west of London. The site was bought in 1514 by Cardinal Wolsey who later presented the building to Henry VIII. One of the oldest features of the palace is a splendid 1540 astronomical clock set in Wolsey's Great Gateway **(1)**. The gateway was later redecorated and named after Anne Boleyn. Henry used to travel up the Thames to Hampton Court in ceremonial barges and disembark at a water-gate where an elaborate summer house was built **(2)**. Elizabeth I, on her accession to the throne, kept up and improved upon her father's gardens. Rare plants — including the tobacco plant and the potato — were brought to her hot-houses by Hawkins, Drake and Raleigh. The Great Hall **(3)**, where lavish plays were presented, is the oldest surviving Elizabethan theatre in England. At the end of the 17th century four new ranges in the classical French Renaissance style were built round the New Fountain Court **(4)** to Sir Christopher Wren's designs. Hampton Court Park and Bushy Park, physically separated by Hampton Court Road **(5)**, were used extensively as hunting reserves by various monarchs from Henry VIII to Victoria. Across Hampton Court Road from the Lion Gates **(6)**, in Bushy Park, stretches a magnificent mile-long avenue of horse-chestnut trees laid out by Sir Christopher Wren on the orders of William III. A large fountain **(7)** surmounted by Diana (the Huntress) stands at the southern end of the avenue. Hampton Court Park is notable for its formal Privy Garden, the Great Vine (planted in 1796) and its celebrated maze **(8)**.

View from the Thames across the Palace towards the Diana Fountain. Note the formal gardens (centre left) and, further left, the glasshouse in which can be found the Great Vine.

The All England Lawn Tennis And Croquet Club – better known as Wimbledon. The enclosed courts are No 1 (left) and the famous Centre Court – scene of so many exciting championships.

View of Richmond in 1981. Comparison with the vertical aerial photograph on page 10 shows clearly the redevelopment of the riverfront down river from Richmond Bridge.

↓ ST MARGARETS

SCALE — 1:10 0000   500 METRES

RICHMOND

The early history of Richmond revolves round the Manor House which was owned by Henry I and named Shene Palace by him in 1125. It was much improved by Richard II, demolished by him in 1394, and rebuilt by Henry VII, who renamed it Richmond. It fell into ruins after 1689, when it ceased to be a royal residence. All that is left of the palace today is the Tudor gateway on Richmond Green **(1)**. The Green has been the centre for pageants and spectacles for centuries and was, in medieval times, a jousting ground. Queen Anne's reign saw some fine building round the Green, and there are also some superb examples of 18th-century houses, notably Old Palace Terrace and Maids of Honour Row. The Green has had a long association with the theatre. The original 'Theatre on the Green' survived until 1884. In 1899 the Theatre Royal and Opera House **(2)** was opened on the Little Green. In the centre of Richmond stands St Mary Magdalen's Church **(3)**, which is made up of a mixture of architectural styles, from Tudor (the tower) to the 20th century. At the end of the 18th century a bridge was built across the Thames to Twickenham **(4)**. Completed in 1777, Richmond Bridge is still one of the prettiest across the river. Upstream from Richmond, on the banks of the Thames, stands magnificent Ham House **(5)**. Built in 1610, its remarkable 17th-century garden has recently been recreated. On the Middlesex bank, opposite Ham House, is Marble Hill **(6)**, built *c.*1720 by George II for his mistress. At the entrance to Richmond Park stands the Star and Garter Home **(7)**, for disabled soldiers and sailors. Richmond Park **(8)** is over 2,350 acres in extent.

SCALE — 1:10 0000   500 METRES

KEW

Kew is situated south of the Thames between Chiswick and Brentford. The Prince of Wales lived in the White House at Kew from 1731 onwards. When this was demolished in 1802 George III moved into Kew Palace **(1)** instead, which had previously served as an annexe to the White House. Kew Palace was built in 1631 for a London merchant. The present 17th-century-style garden behind Kew Palace is named Queen's Garden after Elizabeth II. Kew Gardens, which are a combination of scientific centre and tourist attraction, cover an area of 300 acres (121 hectares). The grounds were extensively altered and improved by Capability Brown around 1770. Their present-day success is due to the eminent 19th-century botanist, Sir Joseph Banks. In 1841 the Botanic Gardens were presented to the nation by means of a Royal Commission. Many of the edifices in the gardens were designed by Sir William Chambers. These include the Temples of Arethusa, Bellona **(2)** and Aeolus, the impressive Orangery **(3)** and the Chinese Pagoda **(4)**. Of Decimus Burton's great glasshouses, there is the conventional Temperate House **(5)** and the splendid curved glass structure of the Palm House **(6)**. To the west of Kew Gardens stands Syon House **(7)**. This stone-built turreted quadrangle was home to the Dukes of Northumberland from 1594. It has many royal and historical connections, and displays the work of Robert Adam at its best. The lovely grounds of Syon Park were laid out by Capability Brown. The Great Conservatory was designed by Charles Fowler and houses one of the finest private collections of tropical plants in the country.

Decimus Burton's Temperate House with, to the left, Australia House.

Sir William Chambers's Chinese Pagoda, inspired by a visit to China in his youth. The pagoda stands ten storeys – some 163ft – high.

CHISWICK

About 6 miles (9.6km) west of Hyde Park Corner, Chiswick is situated in a sweeping bend of the Thames with Hammersmith to the east and Brentford to the west. Until the mid-19th century Chiswick was a rural area comprised of large estates. One such, Chiswick House **(1)**, is a country-styled villa and was the home of the Dukes of Devonshire

until they moved to Chatsworth. Although Chiswick has never been industrial, the small local brewery, started some 300 years ago, has now developed into the large Fuller, Smith and Turner Brewery **(2)**. Just across the A4 trunk road from the brewery stands Hogarth's House **(3)**, the artist's country retreat for 15 years until his death in 1764. It was first opened as a museum in 1909. Following the bend of the

Thames, Chiswick Mall and Upper Mall Hammersmith make a very pleasant walk or bike ride, with several fine pubs looking out to the river. Many of the oldest houses in Chiswick, some predating the 17th century, stand in Chiswick Mall **(4)**. Kelmscott House, where Sir Francis Ronalds lived and invented the electric telegraph, stands in Upper Mall **(5)**. William Morris subsequently lived there and established his

14

⬇ Page 16

Chiswick House, a haven of peace just off the Great West Road.

printing and design works in the house. Built in 1824-7, Hammersmith Bridge **(6)** was the first suspension bridge in London. It was replaced by the present bridge in 1883-7 using the original piers and abutments. To combat the increased weight of traffic it had new deck girders installed in a major overhaul in the 1970s.

15

← HAMMERSMITH ⊖

→ HAMMERSMITH

OLYMPIA AND EARLS COURT

➜ Page 22

⬥ EARL'S COURT

⬥ WEST BROMPTON

➜ Page 26

To the west of the borough of Kensington and Chelsea lies Olympia **(1)**, one of London's largest exhibition halls. It opened in the 1880s and was originally used as a site for circuses and similar spectacles. In 1895 the Grand Hall was extended and the first Motor Show was held there in 1905; in 1923 the National Hall was built, and in 1929 the Empire Hall. It has been a regular venue for horse, dog and sporting events, although today the larger exhibitions are staged at Earls Court, with Olympia holding the smaller ones and conferences. Hammersmith Broadway **(2)** has always been one of the biggest road junctions in west London — a place where the south-north routes from the river joined and crossed the Great West Road. Today Hammersmith flyover **(3)**, an impressive four-lane structure, helps to alleviate traffic congestion. Just north of the Broadway on the Shepherds Bush Road, stands the *Palais de Danse* — the Hammersmith Palais **(4)**. To the south of the Broadway, almost under the flyover, stands the Hammersmith Odeon **(5)**. Although still used as a cinema, it is more widely known as a rock venue. To the south of the flyover, on the Fulham Palace Road, stands the Charing Cross Hospital **(6)**. Built on the site of the old Fulham Hospital and opened in 1973, it is one of the most modern teaching hospitals in London. East of the Hammersmith flyover, to the south of the A4, lies the Earls Court Exhibition Centre **(7)**, at the time of its opening in 1937 the largest reinforced concrete building in Europe. Today it is the venue for the largest commercial exhibitions in London.

Olympia from the north-east.

ST JOHN'S WOOD ⊖

⬆ MARYLEBONE ⇄ ⊖   ⬆ BAKER STREET ⊖

↑ Page 30

REGENT'S PARK ⊖ ↑ ↑ GREAT PORTLAND STREET

↓ Page 32

REGENT'S PARK

Although its use as a hunting ground dates back to Henry VIII, Regent's Park as we know it today was created as part of the Prince Regent's grand design for a neo-classical development, under the brilliant guidance of John Nash – hence Regent's Park. In 1827 the northern area of the park was laid out for the zoo **(1)**. Throughout the 1960s and 1970s new buildings were added, and London Zoo became one of the biggest tourist attractions in the capital, as well as a centre for research. However, it is the only major zoo in the world which receives no support from central or local government and, as a result, is under a very real threat of closure. Pleasure boat trips are available from the zoo to Little Venice near Warwick Road tube station. The boats make

Regent's Park looking northwards. At the top, nestling in the corner of the Park, is London Zoo. In the foreground can be seen the Boating Lake and Queen Mary's Gardens.

use of the Regent's Canal **(2)** which follows the Outer Circle round the park's northern and western perimeters, continuing through Camden to join the Thames at Limehouse Basin. In an anti-clockwise direction round the Outer Circle from the zoo stands the magnificent Central London Mosque with its gold roof **(3)**. Continuing in the same direction, Cornwall Terrace **(4)**, which forms part of the southern boundary of the Park, was the first of the Nash terraces built in the Park – c.1820; part of it now houses the British Academy. Although Regent's

Continued on page 20.

19

HYDE PARK

Hyde Park **(1)** covers an area of over 340 acres (138 hectares). It stretches from the Bayswater Road in the north to Knightsbridge in the south, and from Park Lane **(2)** in the east to where it merges with Kensington Gardens in the west. The boundary between Kensington Gardens **(3)** and Hyde Park follows a line from Alexander Gate **(4)** in the south, over Serpentine Bridge **(5)**, and up Buck Hill Walk to Victoria Gate **(6)** in the north. Like most of the royal parks, Hyde Park was originally used for hunting but was opened to the public at the beginning of the 17th century.

When William III came to live at Kensington Palace **(7)** at the end of the 17th century he had 300 lamps hung from the trees along the *route du roi* (which came to be known as Rotten Row) **(8)**. It was the first road in England to be lit at night and was meant as a deterrent to highwaymen. Originally a Jacobean mansion, Kensington Palace was reconstructed by Wren and Hawksmoor on the orders of William and Mary. Queen Mary took a great interest in the gardens but later Queen Anne, who did not like the formal Dutch gardens, had them uprooted and new plans drawn up: The gardens are today pretty much the same as those early 18th-century plans depicted. To the south of Kensington Gardens stands the Albert Memorial **(9)** — a national memorial to Prince Albert, Consort to Queen Victoria. The memorial was designed by Sir Gilbert Scott and erected 1863-76. It stands directly opposite the Royal Albert Hall **(10)**. Originally meant to be the 'Hall of Arts and Sciences', it was Victoria who prefaced it with 'Royal Albert' during the laying of the foundation stone.

Park suffered severe bomb damage during the Second World War and neglect afterwards, there was a great will and determination to restore it to its former glory. By the late 1970s, with the refurbishment of the eastern boundary of the Park including Gloucester, Cumberland and Chester Terraces **(5)**, the rehabilitation was complete. The total area of Regent's Park bounded by the Outer Circle is 487 acres (197 hectares). In the centre of the Park, within the boundaries of the Inner Circle **(6)**, lies Queen Mary's Gardens, with the Open Air Theatre at the northern perimeter. From 1839 to 1932 the Gardens belonged to the Royal Botanic Society. To the west of Regent's Park, in St John's Wood Road, stands Lord's cricket ground **(7)**, the spiritual home of English cricket. Although a modern Test Cricket venue, the old part of the pavilion is steeped in the history of the sport and houses a museum

Lord's – home of Middlesex County Cricket Club, Marylebone Cricket Club and world cricket

The gleaming gold roof of the Central London Mosque.

dedicated to the game. Just south of the Park, standing almost side by side on the Marylebone Road, are the tourist attractions of Madame Tussauds **(8)** and the Planetarium **(9)**.

Hyde Park Corner looking towards Marble Arch. The gardens at the bottom of the picture belong to Buckingham Palace. The brown-faced building in the centre of the photograph is Apsley House – the home of Arthur Wellesley, Duke of Wellington. Presented to the nation in 1947, it became the Wellington Museum in 1952. To the left of Apsley House is Decimus Burton's grand park entrance and, in the square in front, his Constitution Arch.

Marble Arch. In the foreground is the top of Park Lane with its tree-lined central reservation. To the bottom left is Speakers' Corner, at the top of Hyde Park.

The Serpentine and Long Water.

⊕ ↓ QUEENSWAY

SCALE – 1:10 0000   500 METRES

➡ Page 32

➡ Page 36

⬅ HYDE PARK CORNER ⊖

The distinctive rotunda building of the Royal Albert Hall. In the foreground can be seen the pinnacles of the Albert Memorial.

Harrods – the world famous department store with its renowned frontage.

Kensington Palace.

Grosvenor Square with the American Embassy standing on the west side. The British memorial to Franklin D. Roosevelt can be seen in the square.

↑ FULHAM BROADWAY ⊕

SCALE — 1:10 0000　　500 METRES

KENSINGTON AND CHELSEA

Some of London's best-known museums, including the Natural History Museum **(1)**, the Geological Museum **(2)**, the Science Museum **(3)** and the Victoria and Albert Museum **(4)** lie within a short walk of one another. The laying of the foundation stone of the Victoria and Albert Museum was the last important public engagement by Queen Victoria. It was not, however, until 1909 that this imposing terracotta brick building was officially opened by Edward VII. To the south-west of the museums lies the Brompton Cemetery **(5)**. Its original design with several chapels and 'long arms' of catacombs reaching out to form a 'Great Circle' was never fully realised, but it remains an interesting site. In 1852 it became the first London cemetery to come under state control, and in 1980 was laid out as a public place. Among those buried here are Emmeline Pankhurst the Suffragette and Sir Henry Cole, the organising genius behind the Great Exhibition and the Victoria and Albert Museum. Standing beside the cemetery is Stamford Bridge **(6)**, home of Chelsea Football Club. To the east of Stamford Bridge, running alongside the Thames, is Cheyne Walk **(7)**. This features beautiful Queen Anne and Georgian houses where many of the rich and famous traditionally reside. This part of the Thames also contains a thriving houseboat community. When built in 1722 the original Battersea Bridge was the only bridge between Westminster and Putney. It transformed Chelsea from a hamlet to a small town. The current bridge **(8)** was built in 1886-90.

The Victoria and Albert Museum as seen from the Cromwell Road. On Exhibition Road, running at right-angles, are Imperial College, the Science and the Geological Museums.

Looking over Kensington towards the Albert Hall and Hyde Park. The copper-topped tower stands in the court of the Imperial College of Science and Technology.

BELGRAVIA AND CHELSEA

Battersea Park **(1)** was opened in 1853, and by the end of the 19th century had become a meeting place for those who had succumbed to the new craze of bicycling — a pastime for which it is still popular today. Across the Thames from Battersea Park, in a triangle formed by Chelsea Embankment to the south, Royal Hospital Road to the west and Chelsea Bridge Road to the east, lies the Chelsea Royal Hospital **(2)**, founded by Charles II in 1682 as a home for veteran soldiers. The Chelsea Pensioners' uniforms, the distinctive scarlet tunics and the three-cornered hats, date from the 18th century. The King's Road **(3)**, which was once Charles II's private carriage route to Hampton Court, is today a lively and exciting thoroughfare. Since the 1960s it has been known for the chic fashion boutiques which stand side-by-side with shops selling goods dating from the 1950s to the very latest styles. The King's Road runs east into Sloane Square **(4)**, which was named after Sir Hans Sloane, Lord of the Manor of Chelsea. In the centre of the square stands the Venus Fountain, winner of a Royal Academy award for fountains. The east side of the square is taken up by the Royal Court Theatre built in 1888 and remodelled in 1965. Many of Shaw's early plays were performed here at the beginning of this century. Albert Bridge **(5)** is a hybrid construction featuring elements of both cantilever and suspension. It was overhauled in 1991 and is illuminated at night by hundreds of lights. The original cast iron Chelsea Bridge **(6)**, built 1851-8, was replaced by the current suspension bridge in 1934.

Chelsea Royal Hospital – the east and west wings house the quarters of the famous Chelsea Pensioners.

The Royal Hospital from the west, looking towards Hyde Park. Note Victoria Station on the right.

↑ CALEDONIAN ROAD AND BARNSBURY ↑

↑ KING'S CROSS

⬇ Page 33

CAMDEN TOWN

Camden Town, as described in the Domesday Book, was originally an area of 'rural lanes, hedgeside roads and lovely fields'. With a stretch of the Regent's Canal constructed through it in the early part of the 19th century, bringing with it coal wharves and merchants and some light industry, Camden Town ceased to be rural. Since the Second World War the face of Camden Town has changed again. There has been large-scale redevelopment and with it a steady return of residents from the professional classes. Camden Lock (1), on the Regent's Canal, boasts a very colourful and exotic market, with a profusion of ethnic restaurants and lively bars in the surrounding area. Just south of Camden Town stand three main-line railway stations, Euston (2), St Pancras (3) and King's Cross (4). Euston, opening in 1837, is both the oldest and,

St Pancras station. To the left is the massive construction site of the new British Library.

with its recent comprehensive rebuilding, the newest of London's main-line railway stations. The original Midland Grand Hotel (1868-72) forms the amazing façade of St Pancras station. George Gilbert Scott's Gothic design has high pinnacles, towers and gables. It was closed as a hotel in the 1930s and is now used as offices. King's Cross station (1851-2) was the biggest station in England when it opened. It was named after a monument to George IV which stood on a crossroads near the site. Between St Pancras and Euston is the site of the new British Library (5) buildings. With the completion of the project all the diverse operations of the Library will be brought under one roof.

⊖ GREAT PORTLAND STREET ↓

⊖ GOODGE STREET ↓

⊖ OXFORD CIRCUS ↓

SCALE — 1:8000   500 METRES

➡ HOLBORN ⊕

⬇ Page 44

➡ ALDWYCH ⊕

⬆ COVENT GARDEN ⊖   ⬇ Page 37

BLOOMSBURY AND SOHO

University College **(1)**, in Gower Street, was founded in 1826 to provide university education for those non-Anglicans who were refused entry to Oxford or Cambridge. It was incorporated into the University of London in 1907. The area of London known as Bloomsbury — once the preserve of the scholars, artists and writers of the Bloomsbury Group — is now dominated by University of London buildings and the British Museum **(2)**. To the south-west of Bloomsbury lies Soho. This most cosmopolitan area of London is bounded by Oxford Street from Tottenham Court Road **(3)** to Oxford Circus **(4)**, Regent Street, running from Oxford Circus to Piccadilly Circus, Shaftesbury Avenue from Piccadilly Circus to Cambridge Circus **(5)**, and Charing Cross Road (from Cambridge Circus to Tottenham Court Road). It became London's principal foreign quarter in the late 17th century when thousands of French Protestant refugees were forced to leave France after the Revocation of the Edict of Nantes. East of Soho and to the south of Bloomsbury is the Covent Garden area **(6)**. Since the famous fruit and vegetable market moved to its new site in 1974, complete restoration has transformed Covent Garden into an attractive area of specialist shops and eating places. In the summer months a wide variety of street entertainers and musicians perform here. The Royal Opera House **(7)**, standing at the north-east corner of Covent Garden, has been host to the world's top opera and ballet stars in its renowned lavish productions. The London Transport Museum **(8)** can be found in the south-east corner.

British Telecom – formerly the GPO – Tower. The revolving restaurant just below the Telecom lettering can no longer be visited.

Centre Point office block with the church of St Giles-in-the-Field to its right.

Lincoln's Inn Fields and Gray's Inn (top right), one of the other Inns of Court.

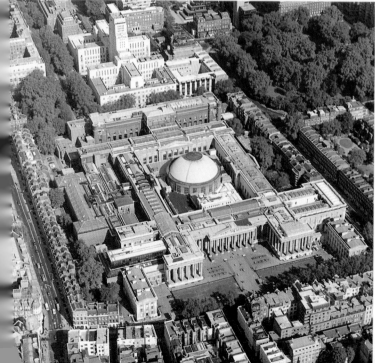

View of Bloomsbury with, in the foreground, Russell Square. At the centre is the dome of the British Museum's reading room and, to the right, Senate House. Behind the museum is Bedford Square and Centre Point.

The British Museum, with Gower Street to the left and Russell Square to the right.

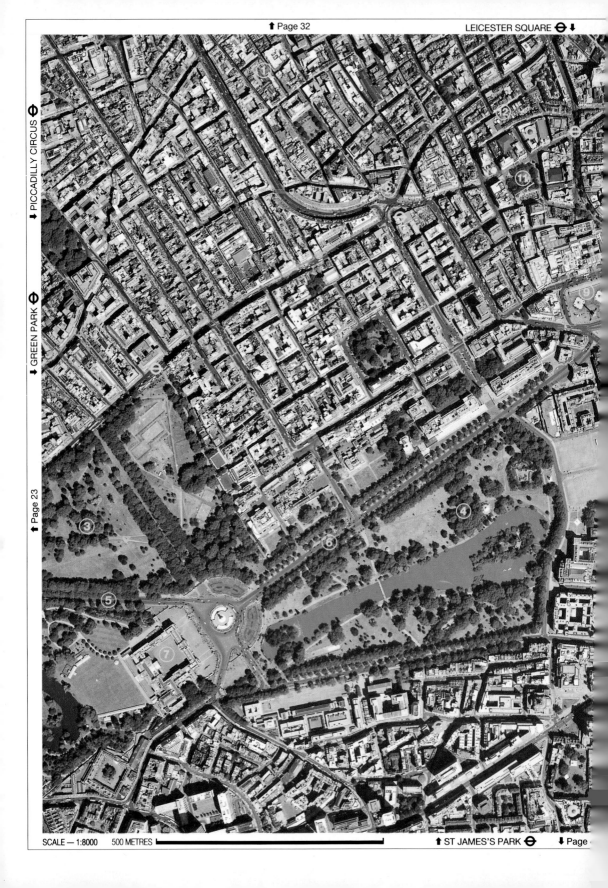

⊕ PICCADILLY CIRCUS

⊕ GREEN PARK

↑ Page 23

↑ CHARING CROSS

EMBANKMENT ⊖ ↑

↓ Page 50

THE WEST END

Tucked away near Regent Street, Carnaby Street **(1)** was the focal point of popular London fashion throughout the 'Swinging Sixties'. To the south lies Piccadilly Circus **(2)**, with its famous statue of Eros. This symbolic memorial fountain, erected in memory of the philanthropic 7th Earl of Shaftesbury, was originally intended to represent the Angel of Christian Charity, and not Eros, the God of Love. South of Piccadilly Circus lies Green Park **(3)** and St James's Park **(4)**, separated by Constitution Hill **(5)** and the Mall **(6)**. Green Park is said to have been the burial ground for lepers from nearby St James's Hospital, which is supposedly why there are no flowers in it. It was enclosed by Henry VIII and turned into a royal park by Charles II. St James's Park, the oldest of the Royal Parks, has Buckingham Palace and its gardens **(7)** at its western perimeter. George IV employed Nash to transform Buckingham House into a palace in 1825, but it was not much used until the middle of the 19th century, by which time Queen Victoria had grown to love the building. Along the Mall from Buckingham Palace, on the north side of St James's Park, stands St James's Palace **(8)**. Built by Henry VIII, the Palace remained one of the principal residences of the monarchs of England for over 300 years. To this day, the accession of a new sovereign is still initially proclaimed at St James's Palace. At the other end of the Mall from Buckingham Palace, through Admiralty Arch, is Trafalgar Square **(9)**. Dominated by its 145ft (44m)-high Nelson Column, the square was laid out in honour of Lord Nelson to commemorate his last and greatest victory, Trafalgar. It has long been the

Continued on page 38.

meeting place for political demonstrations, and today is often the terminal point for marches. The north side of the Square is taken up by the National Gallery **(10)**, which houses many of Britain's art treasures. Northwards, up the Charing Cross Road from Trafalgar Square, is Leicester Square **(11)**, which has changed radically in the last hundred years from an area of opulent houses to a fairly characterless one dominated by cinemas and snack bars. Just north, Gerrard Street forms the main part of London's Chinatown **(12)**. East from Trafalgar Square is the Strand **(13)**, originally a bridle path running alongside the river, hence the name. A street with shops, hotels, theatres and restaurants, it is one of the main links between the West End and the City of London. In the 1890s the Strand contained more theatres than any other street in London, but today only three remain — the Savoy, the Adelphi and the Vaudeville.

Covent Garden, once London's flower and vegetable market. The London Transport Museum is sited at the bottom of the piazza, at the top Inigo Jones's church.

Piccadilly Circus with its famous electronic advertising hoardings. Regent Street curves away to the left.

WESTMINSTER

Running south from Trafalgar Square is Whitehall, in which stands the Cenotaph **(14)**. Devoid of any religious symbols, this is a national memorial to the 'Glorious Dead' of both World Wars. Almost directly opposite the Cenotaph is Downing Street **(15)** where, since 1732, Number 10 has been the official residence of the Prime Minister. The southern end of Whitehall runs into Parliament Square **(16)**. Between Parliament Square and the River Thames stands the Palace of Westminster **(17)**. A fire in 1834 destroyed most of the medieval old palace, in various buildings of which

Parliament had met since the early 16th century. Sir Charles Barry's great Perpendicular Gothic replacement building was completed in the middle of the 19th century, providing a building worthy of being the Houses of Parliament. Barry's structure stood intact for nearly a century, but in May 1941 the House of Commons was reduced to rubble by the *Luftwaffe*. It was rebuilt in the tradition of the old Chamber and was completed in 1950. On the south side of Parliament Square, across the road from the Palace of Westminster, stands

Westminster Abbey **(18)**. A substantial foundation of the Abbey undoubtedly existed in 1040 when Edward the Confessor became king. The whole Abbey was rebuilt in his honour from 1245-69, and altered and added to through succeeding centuries. The Abbey is crowded with tombs and monuments to royalty, statesmen, soldiers, poets, artists and all manner of famous historical figures. One of the most visited tombs is that of the 'Unknown Soldier', whose body was brought back from France after the First World War.

Trafalgar Square looking north towards the National Gallery. Leicester Square can be seen top left, and the church of St Martin-in-the-Fields centre right.

St James's Palace from St James's Park. The Mall can be seen in the foreground.

Westminster Abbey with the Foreign Office on the opposite side of Parliament Square. The Cenotaph can be seen to the right in Whitehall.

The Houses of Parliament with the clock tower known as Big Ben. Behind is the Foreign Office, and Trafalgar Square and the Nelson Column can be seen at the top of Whitehall.

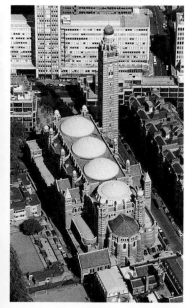

Westminster Cathedral, clearly showing the contrasting bands of Portland stone used in its construction.

The Tate Gallery, repository of much of the nation's modern art.

Lambeth Palace and its gardens, official residence of the Archbishop of Canterbury.

WESTMINSTER AND LAMBETH

Just to the south of Victoria Street **(1)**, which runs westwards from Parliament Square, stands Westminster Cathedral **(2)**. This Roman Catholic cathedral is of an Early Christian Byzantine style of architecture and has the widest nave in England. The interior is ornamented with more than 100 different kinds of marble quarried from all over the world. Although the fabric of the building was completed in 1903, the decoration of the interior, with all its mosaics, continues today. Not far from Westminster Cathedral, running down to Lambeth Bridge **(3)**, is Horseferry Road **(4)**, named after the only horse ferry allowed on the Thames near London. The horse ferry is believed to have been even older than London Bridge, the first bridge built across the Thames in London. The right

42

The Imperial War Museum surrounded by the Geraldine Mary Harmsworth Park Gardens.

grew up in the 19th century and was well-established by the 1840s. The street was made famous by a cockney dance in the 1937 musical *Me and My Gal*. To the east of Lambeth Palace, across the Kennington Road, is the Imperial War Museum **(7)**, which collects, preserves and displays material and information relating to all the military operations that Great Britain and the Commonwealth have been involved in since 1914. The building which houses the museum was previously the Bethlehem Royal Hospital (Bedlam). Up-river from Lambeth Palace and to the east of Vauxhall Bridge **(8)** is the Kennington Oval **(9)**, headquarters of the Surrey County Cricket Club. The first Test Match between England and Australia was played at the Oval in September 1880. Many other sports have also been played here, including rugby and association football. Most of the Football Association Cup Finals were held here between 1870 and 1892. During the Second World War the Oval was used as a prisoner-of-war camp. The Tate Gallery **(10)** opened in 1897 and is known today for its modern collection.

o collect tolls for the ferry belonged to the Archbishops of Canterbury, whose official residence was Lambeth Palace **(5)** on the south bank of the Thames beside Lambeth Bridge. Records of building on the site of Lambeth Palace date back to the late 12th century. Between 1828-34 the structure was rebuilt, with the residential part of the palace being completely reconstructed in the Gothic style. The first Lambeth conference, attended by Bishops from all over the world, was held in 1867; conferences are still held here today. South of Lambeth Palace is Lambeth Walk **(6)**, a busy general street market open seven days a week. This market

⬆ Page 33

⬅ CHANCERY LANE ⊖

SCALE — 1:8000   500 METRES

↕ MOORGATE

↓ Page 54

↕ BANK

↕ MONUMENT

THE CITY

Gray's Inn (1), founded in the middle of the 14th century, is one of the four Inns of Court. It is believed that the inns came into existence for the education and lodging of students of law and barristers. In 1852 the Council of Legal Education was set up and by 1872 compulsory examinations for students at the bar were held. The other inns are Lincoln's Inn (Holborn) and the Inner and Middle Temples (2). To the east of Gray's Inn, running between Clerkenwell Road and Holborn Circus (3), is Hatton Garden (4), the centre of the London diamond trade. Nearby in Holborn Viaduct (5) are De Beers, through whom 80 per cent of the world's diamond production is sold. Holborn Viaduct was completed in 1869 to bridge the Fleet river valley. Running south from the viaduct is Old Bailey (6), the street which gives its name to the Central Criminal Court there. The first Old Bailey Sessions House in regular use dates back to the middle of the 16th century. The southern end of Old Bailey joins Ludgate Hill (7), named after the Lud Gate which, tradition says, was built by King Lud in 66BC. At the junction of Ludgate Hill and Fleet Street (8) is Ludgate Circus. In a house near the old bridge, where Fleet Street crossed the River Fleet, the first daily newspaper was published in 1702. Smithfield meat market (9) was known in the Middle Ages for its horse market; the existing structure was opened in 1868. Designed by Henry Jones, it was modelled on Paxton's Crystal Palace. At the top of Ludgate Hill stands St Paul's Cathedral (10), the fifth cathedral to be built on the site. The present St Paul's was designed by Sir Christopher Wren after the Great Fire had all but destroyed the previous building.

Continued on page 46.

45

The foundation stone was laid in 1675 and the cathedral completed in 1710. The beautiful, great central dome which Wren envisaged instead of the usual tall steeple, although posing him considerable constructional problems, proved to be a supreme example of his genius, and is today one of London's most famous landmarks. Sir Christopher Wren is buried in the crypt of the cathedral, as is Lord Nelson and the Duke of Wellington. Despite its vulnerability, St Paul's remained remarkably unscathed during the fierce incendiary bomb attacks in its vicinity during the Second World War. To the east of St Paul's, along Cheapside, stands the 'Old Lady of Threadneedle Street' — The Bank of England **(11)**. This magnificent neo-classical building, surrounded by a windowless wall, was greatly reconstructed by Sir John Soane at

The City. The Lloyd's Building (see page 55) is in the centre with blue cranes on top; the tallest tower is the National Westminster building.

The Barbican and, top left, the long building of Smithfield meat market.

46

the end of the 18th century. The main functions of the Bank today include managing the National Debt, authorising the issue of notes and custodianship of the nation's gold reserves. South-west of the Bank stands the Mansion House **(12)**, official residence of the Lord Mayor of London during his year of office. The foundation stone was laid in 1739, but few of the original fittings survived Victorian alterations. There was a general restoration of the whole structure during the 1930s, refurnishing it to its original style. Almost adjacent to the Bank of England is the Stock Exchange **(13)**. Although joint stock companies first appeared in the mid-16th century the present building, opened in 1972, stands on a site which the Exchange has occupied since 1801. No stranger is allowed on the floor of the Exchange but visitors can watch the conduct of business from the public gallery. North of the Bank and to the west of Moorgate stands the Barbican **(14)**, named after an outer fortification of the City. The site, an area laid waste by the bombs of the Second World War, was bought by the City of London and the County Council in 1958. It was proposed that 'a genuine residential neighbourhood including schools, shops and open spaces and amenities' should be created. Amidst the 400ft (122m)-high residential tower blocks, are also pubs, offices, the Guildhall School of Music, the Museum of London and the Barbican Centre of Arts and Conferences. Officially opened by the Queen in March 1982, this includes an art gallery, three cinemas, a concert hall and a ,166-seat theatre. To the east of the Barbican, between Moorgate and London Wall, is Finsbury Circus Garden **(15)**, a popular lunchtime rendezvous for City people.

The 'Old Lady of Threadneedle Street' – the Bank of England. The flat, six-sided roof of the Stock Exchange is to the right of the Bank.

The Lloyd's Building with, bottom left, the top of Leadenhall Market, a wonderful Victorian covered market now full of shops.

St Paul's Cathedral.

Gray's Inn, one of the four inns of court. It was named after the landowners in the 14th century.

The medieval Guildhall was severely damaged in the Great Fire (1666) and later in the Blitz (1940), but much of the original building remains today.

The Law Courts on the Strand. In front of and to the left of the Courts is the RAF church of St Clement Danes.

↓ WATERLOO EAST ⊷

WATERLOO ⊖ ⊷

↑ Page 37

SOUTHWARK

This stretch of the Thames includes the three 'City' road bridges — Blackfriars **(1)**, Southwark **(2)** and London Bridge **(3)**. The original Blackfriars Bridge, the third bridge (1760-9) to span the Thames in London, was replaced in the 1860s by the present wrought iron and granite structure. It was opened by Queen Victoria on the same day as Holborn Viaduct. Southwark Bridge was originally constructed in the early part of the 19th century due to demand for an extra river crossing between Blackfriars and London Bridge; the present bridge dates from the early 20th century. The original London Bridge, the first bridge across the Thames in London, was probably built between 100AD and 400AD during the Roman occupation. In 1305 the head of Scots patriot William Wallace was put up above the portico of the gatehouse, so beginning a gruesome custom which continued into the 17th century. Through the centuries London Bridge has been rebuilt many times; between 1967 and 1972 the present bridge was built replacing the 1820s five-arch stone structure which, sold and re-erected, now stands as a tourist attraction in Arizona, USA. To the north of Waterloo Station **(4)** and west of Blackfriars Bridge stands the National Theatre **(5)**. The National, with its three theatres — the Cottesloe, the Lyttleton and the Olivier — forms part of the 'South Bank' arts complex, which also includes the Royal Festival Hall, the Museum of the Moving Image (MOMI), the Queen Elizabeth Hall and the National Film Theatre. As the main entry to London from the south-east, Southwark had always been a lively bustling area, though never rivalling the City. It has been

Continued on page 52.

51

renowned since Chaucer's time for its strong ales, and many breweries were established here. One of the largest, Barclay & Perkins (now merged with Courage), stands on the site believed to have been occupied by Shakespeare's Globe Theatre (6). The George Inn (7), the only galleried coaching inn left in London and now owned and preserved by the National Trust, was built in 1676 on the site of, and as an exact replica of, a medieval inn. One of Southwark's many celebrated hostelries, the George remained an important terminus for coaches and mail into the 19th century. In the summer Shakespeare plays are performed in the yard. Adjacent to the George is Talbot Yard, the site of the original Tabard Inn — the meeting place of Chaucer's Pilgrims.

'In Southwark at the Tabard as I lay
Ready to wende on my pilgrimage'.

In the 17th century the street still named Bankside (8) was described as a 'continued ale-house'; it also contained one of Southwark's

seven prisons – the most notorious of these was Clink in Clink Street, now a museum. Southwark Cathedral (9), at the southern approach to London Bridge, is one of the City's finest Gothic buildings – despite being altered and restored over the centuries. The diocese of Southwark was created in 1905. Adjacent to Southwark Cathedral is London Bridge mainline railway station (10). In the vaults below the station is the London Dungeon, a waxworks horror museum.

Southwark Cathedral.

The South Bank Complex: Hungerford Bridge (railway) on the right; the Royal Festival Hall; Waterloo Bridge; the National Theatre; then Blackfriars road and rail bridges.

TOWER BRIDGE

Along with St Paul's Cathedral, the Houses of Parliament and the Nelson Column, Tower Bridge (1) must be one of London's most familiar landmarks. Until November 1991, when the Queen Elizabeth Bridge at Dartford was opened, Tower Bridge was the only span across the Thames below London Bridge. Opened by the Prince of Wales in 1894, it has an opening span of 200ft (61m) clear width and a headroom of 135ft (41m) to allow ships upstream from the Upper Pool (2). The two towers contain lifts to convey pedestrians to the high level footbridge which was used when it first opened. On the Thames just upstream from Tower Bridge lies HMS *Belfast* (3). The ship, built in 1939 at 11,000 tons, was the largest cruiser ever built for the Royal Navy; she was opened to the public in 1971. On the north bank of the Thames just downstream from Tower Bridge is St Katharine's Dock (4). The docks, which were opened in 1828, were never a major commercial success and since their closure in 1968, the magnificent warehouses have been restored and adapted for a variety of uses. Imaginative redevelopment has brought new life to the area now occupied by the World Trade Centre, the Tower Hotel, a yacht marina and a ship museum displaying a collection of historic vessels. In the gardens of Trinity Square (5), on the west side of the northern approach to Tower Bridge, a stone in the pavement marks the principal execution site of traitors imprisoned in the Tower. Beheadings were carried out here for nearly 360 years, from Sir Simon de Burley (tutor to Richard II) in 1388 to Jacobite Lord Lovat in 1747.

Continued on page 55.

The Tower of London with Trinity Square just to the right. The shadow of Tower Bridge can be seen on the river.

Behind St Katharine's Dock and Tower Bridge, with the Tower to the right, is HMS Belfast, *and the other City river bridges – London Bridge, Cannon Street railway bridge, Southwark Bridge and then Blackfriars bridges.*

↑ Page 45

↑ Page 51

↑ SHADWELL ⊖

↑ WAPPING ⊖

The Tower of London **(6)** was begun by William I, soon after the Battle of Hastings in 1066, and added to by successive monarchs until Edward I completed the outer wall in the late 13th century. The tower soon became the symbol of ultimate power, and has been used as a palace, prison and place for execution. In its time it has housed the royal armouries, the mint, the royal observatory, the royal menagerie, the public records, and today still guards the Crown Jewels. In 1483 the two princes, the young Edward V and his brother Richard, were murdered in the Garden Tower, which was thereafter known as the 'Bloody Tower'. Its most famous prisoner was probably Sir Walter Raleigh, who lived fairly comfortably for 12 years in the upper floors of the Bloody Tower. The famous 'Beefeaters' — Yeoman of the Guard — were formed in 1485 when Henry, Earl of Richmond, ascended to the throne as Henry VII. Although a great number of prisoners had been detained in the Tower since its construction, it was not until the Reformation brought Henry VIII's victims there that harsh treatment of prisoners became the norm. James I was the last monarch to use the Tower as a palace. He was interested in the royal menagerie and animal fights were regularly staged there until a small child was killed by a bear in 1609. The last prisoner held in the Tower was Rudolf Hess during the Second World War. He was held for four days in the Lieutenant's Lodgings where, nearly 350 years earlier, Guy Fawkes and his accomplices were interrogated. North-west of the Tower, in the City's Leadenhall Street, is the ultramodern Lloyd's Building **(7)**, headquarters of a unique insurance market. Begun in 1691, Lloyd's of London is a society of underwriters all of whom accept insurance risks with the possibility of losing their own personal fortunes.

SCALE — 1:8000   500 METRES

HAMPSTEAD

Hampstead Heath comprises approximately 800 acres (324 hectares) including Parliament Hill **(1)**. After the Great Fire of 1666, much of the woods of the Heath were cleared to provide timber for the rebuilding of London. In the early 18th century Hampstead spring water, which was widely sold for its health-giving properties, brought fashionable society to the village. The Flask public house **(2)**, first built in 1663 and renovated in 1910, was so named when flasks of Hampstead water were filled here. Hogarth often visited the Flask as did Karl Marx, who is buried just up the road in Highgate Cemetery **(3)**. Jack Straw's Castle **(4)**, a famous old coaching inn named after one of the leaders of the Peasants' Revolt (1381) and patronised by Dickens and Thackeray, was rebuilt in 1964. There was once a racecourse nearby. Also nearby is the Spaniards **(5)**, which has been a tavern since the 16th century and is said to have been used by Dick Turpin. In 1780 a party of Gordon Rioters (petitioners against the repeal of the anti-Roman Catholic legislation), on their way to destroy Kenwood House, were invited in for a drink by the landlord and kept there until a detachment of soldiers arrived and disarmed them. Their rifles can still be seen at the bar. Kenwood House **(6)**, originally built around 1616, was purchased in 1754 by the 1st Earl of Mansfield and transformed for him by Robert Adam into the magnificent mansion that stands today. It was bought by Edward Cecil Guinness (1st Earl of Iveagh) in 1924, and today, open to the public, Kenwood houses the Iveagh Bequest, which includes works by Van Dyck, Gainsborough, Reynolds, Rembrandt, Landseer and Turner.

HAMPSTEAD HEATH

ISLE OF DOGS

CANARY WHARF DLR ➡

HERON QUAYS DLR ➡